OFFICIALLY NOTED

4/19 Light moisture damage. ym

BRAM STOKER
Author of Dracula

World Writers

BRAM STOKER
Author of Dracula

Nancy Whitelaw

MORGAN
REYNOLDS
Incorporated

Greensboro

BRAM STOKER *Author of Dracula*

Photo credits: William Andrew Clark Memorial Library, University of California, Los
Angeles; Rosenbach Museum & Library; Harry Ransom Humanities Research Center Art
Collection, the University of Texas at Austin; Theatre Museum, London; Barbara Belford;
Tennyson Research Centre; Library of Congress; Museum of Modern Art; Bram Stoker
Collection, Shakespeare Centre Library, Stratford-upon-Avon, .

Library of Congress Cataloging-in-Publication Data
Whitelaw, Nancy
    Bram Stoker, author of Dracula / Nancy Whitelaw. —1st ed.
        p. cm. — (World writers)
    Includes bibliographical references and index.
    Summary: A biography of the theatrical manager and prolific author who, among other
achivements, completed the novel "Dracula" in 1897.
    ISBN 1-883846-30-7
        1. Stoker, Bram, 1847-1912—Biography—Juvenile literature. 2. Novelists,
English—19th century—Biography—Juvenile literature. 3. Theatrical managers—Great
Britian—Biography—Juvenile literature. [1. Stoker, Bram, 1847-1912. 2. Authors,
English. 3. Theatrical managers.] I. Title II. Series.
PR6037 . T617Z95 1998
823'.8—dc21
[b]

                                                                    98-24014
                                                                         CIP
                                                                          AC

Printed in the United States of America
First Edition

Dedicated,
To my favorite children's librarian, Camille Guinnane. She serves the children of Chautauqua County (New York) with love and dedication.

I gratefully acknowledge the help and encouragement of Barbara Belford, author of Bram Stoker; *David Lass, president of The Bram Stoker Society; Elizabeth Miller, author of* Reflections on Dracula; *Marion Pringle, Senior Librarian, The Shakespeare Birthplace Trust, and Jeanne Keyes Youngson, president of the Count Dracula Fan Club.*

I also thank the researchers at the Library of Congress, the Rosenbach Museum & Library, the Museum of Modern Art, the Romanian Embassy, and The Shakespeare Centre in Stratford-upon-Avon (England).

J·B
STOKER
247-0436

Contents

Bram Stoker

Chapter One

Imagination Creates a World

—AROUND THIS TIME—

The Big Ben clock tower was built in London.
Florence Nightingale was a nurse in the Crimean War.
Charles Darwin proposed the theory of evolution.
Popular literature included:
Wuthering Heights by Emily Bronte,
David Copperfield by Charles Dickens,
The Woman in White by Wilkie Collins.

No one knew why the little boy was weak, unable to walk. Illness had been a part of his life since his birth in 1847. When two-year-old Abraham Stoker wanted to go anywhere, he didn't crawl or toddle or walk. He rang a bell. Instantly, his mother, Charlotte Stoker, appeared, ready to carry him wherever he wanted to go.

Much of the time, Abraham lay in bed. He listened to his brother, Thornley, and his sister, Matilda, playing outside.

The rumble of trains over the nearby viaduct gave him dreams of faraway places. He listened to whispers of wind and water in Ireland's Dublin Bay just outside his bedroom window. Sometimes he asked to be seated on his window-sill. There he could watch the tides and the clouds. Once in a while, he saw clipper ships.

Ritual was important to Abraham since he was alone so much. He looked forward to the regular arrival of meals, and to the appearance of parents and siblings to help him with the tasks involved in getting up and then again in going to bed.

His brother Tom was born when Abraham was three years old. Mother didn't always hear Abraham's bell after that. Even when she did, she was sometimes too busy to carry him around.

Then his brother Richard was born, and Abraham's bell became even less useful. It was a good day for Abraham when Thornley brought rocks and insects to him, or when Matilda came to his room to draw pictures with him. The bad days were when the doctor came. He and Abraham's mother talked very quietly about the little boy. He heard worry and fear in their voices. He wondered if he was getting sicker. He wondered if he was going to die.

He knew something about dying. When she had time in the evening, Abraham's mother sat by his bed and told him

Bram began to walk at age seven, when this picture was taken.

stories. Some were ages-old Irish tales about characters like vampires, who were female bloodsuckers, and about Irish fairies that kidnapped children to drink their blood. In her storytelling, his mother often mimicked the banshee howl, the wail of a spirit that told of death to come. She described the custom of piling stones on top of a grave to keep a vampire from rising. There was another reason for covering graves with stones: medical students needed cadavers for study, and grave robbing was one way to acquire them.

Some of her stories were true accounts of the Stokers' life and times. These were stories of starvation, disease, and dying. In the 1840s, later called the "hungry forties," year after year of crops had failed. Then a fungus attacked the all-important potato crop. Mother told of emaciated bodies, rotting corpses, abandoned children, separated families. She even told of dogs eating babies.

The Stoker family had escaped the horror because Abraham Stoker, the man for whom little Abraham was named, was a clerk in the Parliament, not dependent on harvests for his wages. He had moved his family from the disease-ridden streets of Dublin to the open air of Clontarf by the sea. They escaped from the immediate horror, but the threat and the memories stayed in their minds forever. Little Abraham relived the stories his mother had told him, and he worried. Would his family decide that they no longer

Charlotte Stoker told Bram stories of bloodsuckers and fairies stealing children.

had time and food for a sickly child? Would they abandon him? Abraham was ever more alone until he found a constant friend—his imagination. Sitting on his window seat, he told himself stories of storms, shipwrecks, sea rescues, pirates, and unknown lands.

Abraham fed his imagination with stories his mother told him about Irish history. Outlaws hanged, their bodies left to rot on the gallows. Suicides buried with stakes in their bodies to keep their spirits from wandering. People drinking the blood of cows for lack of other nourishment. Ill people buried alive to prevent the spread of cholera. Coffin makers on daily rounds looking for business.

The Stokers' love of storytelling went back to early Irish traditions when families sat around peat fires at night, telling and re-telling tales. Some storytellers had earned the honored title of *seanchaid*—professional storyteller—for their skill in the arts of gesture, voice, and timing.

Charlotte Stoker did more for her children than tell them stories. With no formal schooling, she had educated herself and passed on a love of learning to her children. Abraham's first schooling took place at home with his mother as the teacher and his siblings the other students. His sister Matilda and his brother Thornley also helped with the at-home tutoring. Although the family was not rich, they had enough money to buy books, and Abraham read them all.

As a clerk in Parliament, Abraham's father worked in Dublin Castle. The so-called castle was a group of buildings once used as a fortress; another time used as a jail. For Abraham, Sr., the work was as uninspiring as the gray stone buildings. Although a faithful worker, he felt unappreciated and bored. He encouraged his sons to seek beyond public service for a career.

However, there were career advantages in becoming a clerk. One was that his job was secure.

Another advantage was that as a Protestant working for a Protestant majority government, he had contacts with some of the "right" people who could help his sons in their education.

Suddenly, when little Abraham was seven years old, he began to walk. Delighted, but not ready to believe in this miracle, he tested himself frequently by walking as far as he could. Nothing definite is known about the cause or cure for his problem. Very little is known about his emotions during these exciting months as he learned to do what he had only dreamed of as an invalid. Later in life, he touched lightly on this boyhood illness: "This early weakness passed away, and I grew into a strong boy and in time enlarged to the biggest member of my family."

Sometimes the two Abraham Stokers went to the theater together. After the play, they critiqued each performance as though they were writing reviews. The boy and his father discussed plots, performances, and scenery in detail. The younger Abraham envied actors because each one could become a soldier, a king, a slave, or any other character that a role demanded.

When he learned to write, Abraham wrote some fairy tales. He also tried to put down on paper some of the legends his mother had told him and some of her stories about their family. He wrote about the cholera epidemic as she had described to him.

When he was twelve years old, he went to a private day school run by Rev. William Woods in Dublin. There he took courses in classic subjects to prepare for college. Although he had only been walking for five years, he took part in athletics eagerly. He tested his ability by becoming an endurance walker.

He enrolled at Trinity, a highly respected college of the University of Dublin, in 1863. As an invalid child, he had been shy, withdrawn. As a six-foot, two-inch, 175-pound redheaded seventeen-year-old, he was a campus leader. Rugby and football were his favorite sports, and he also swam and rowed. His physical skills earned him an award as athletic champion of the college.

In classes, his work in history and composition earned him silver medals. The poetry of the romantic poets Byron,

Bram first read Walt Whitman's poetry while a student at Trinity College in Dublin.

Keats, and Shelley intrigued him. A night person, he eagerly discussed these poets and other writers in a favorite setting—pubs around the college that served as community meeting rooms for men.

In 1865, his father retired from civil service, dissatisfied with his career. For almost fifty years, he had worked with little praise and just one promotion. He had gone into debt putting his sons through school. Both Thornley and Richard were already working in medical careers, and this left only Abraham and Tom as students. Young Abraham needed money to finish his schooling; he took a year's leave of absence to work in Dublin Castle as a clerk.

Back in school the next year, he re-entered college life eagerly. Reading the poetry of American writer Walt Whitman was a life-changing event for the twenty-one-year-old student.

On the campus, students and instructors argued about Whitman, the poet who wrote in *Leaves of Grass*: "Give me now libidinous joys only,/Give me the drench of my passions, give me life coarse and rank." Some readers called him immoral; others only laughed at him. After just an hour reading *Leaves of Grass*, Abraham Stoker was an avid fan. He read all of Whitman's work that he could find. One poem that especially appealed to him was "Trickle Drops" with its celebration of death: "Trickle Drops! my blue veins leaving!/O drops of me! trickle, slow drops." Over and over, he read lines like "A shroud I see and I am the shroud, I wrap a body and lie in the coffin/It is dark here underground, it is not evil or pain here, it is blank here." Stoker found a hero, perhaps one whose footsteps he could follow.

In keeping with his fascination for words, Stoker enjoyed being part of the Historical Society, a debating group. He learned to think and speak quickly. To him, debating was a lot like acting. The debater, like an actor, focused on capturing and keeping the attention of the audience.

One of the requirements for belonging to the Historical Society was to present papers to the group. Carrying on the tradition he and his father had enjoyed of critiquing plays, Stoker critiqued literature. In his paper, "Fictionalism and Society," he declared that novels were increasingly immoral. This was a declaration in tune with the strict Victorian beliefs of his time that advocated rigid rules of behavior and thought.

Families often read together, and many pious Victorian individuals saw family reading as a reason to censor literature. Popular works like those of Shakespeare contained vocabulary and ideas judged to be offensive to women and children. For example, the speech of a drunken porter was cut from *Macbeth*; the word belly was changed to body in several plays; in Thomas Hardy's *Tess of the d'Urbervilles*, a seduction scene was changed to a mock marriage.

Chapter Two

The Theater Calls

—AROUND THIS TIME—

Education became compulsory in England.
Louis Pasteur published his theory of germs.
"Sensational" novels were serialized in magazines.
Popular literature included:
Little Women by Louisa May Alcott,
Anna Karenina by Leo Tolstoy,
Les Miserables by Victor Hugo.

In 1867, an event occurred that changed Stoker's life forever. He saw actor Henry Irving on stage playing a soldier who put his life on the line for his integrity. Stoker recognized in Irving the same attributes he had recognized in Whitman—passion for his career, excellence in his performance, and the ability to charm his audiences. Stoker had a new hero. Irving became a role model in his life. The young student entered some auditions for acting parts and won a few small parts.

However, most of his attention was on Trinity. He still enjoyed debating, discussing literature, attending plays. Stoker was a night person, and often was one of the last to leave a pub after a lively discussion.

In 1871, Irving's performance in the comedy *Two Roses* so enchanted Stoker that he saw the play three times. He was upset that no mention was made of the play in the leading Dublin paper, the *Evening Mail*. Then he saw Irving star in *The Bells*, the story of a man who murders for money. The murderer is forever after haunted by the sounds of the bells on his victim's sleigh. Again, the *Evening Mail* made no mention of Irving's performance. Stoker offered to become drama critic for the paper.

The editor accepted his offer. Stoker received no pay and no by-line. What he did receive was far more important to him—a ticket to each performance. He became comfortable backstage, chatting with the cast and studying scenery, costumes, and props. Unlike some critics, Stoker always read a play before he saw it. Readers appreciated his reviews.

An interesting sidelight to this "job" was Stoker's acquaintance with Sheridan Le Fanu, joint-owner of the *Evening Mail*. Le Fanu was a popular writer of horror tales. One of his more famous stories, "Carmilla," told of a six-year-old girl who was bitten by a vampire. Stoker enjoyed Le Fanu's gripping tales of nightmares, ghosts, haunted houses, and supernaturalism.

Twenty-four-year-old Bram graduated in 1871 with a degree in science. He had no definite plans for his future. His father, mother, and sisters had moved to France where Abraham Sr.'s pension would stretch further. His brother Tom was still a student, and his other brothers were busy with medical careers.

Unwilling to leave the college scene entirely, he decided to study for a master's degree in mathematics. He took classes during the day and worked at night to support himself and to pay tuition costs. It seemed natural and easy, although not particularly attractive, for him to return to Dublin Castle as a clerk.

As a young boy, he had dreamed of shipwrecks, pirates, and travel to faraway places. As a college student, he had immersed himself in athletics, debating, late nights at the pubs. Now as a young man, he could not be content with a desk job that offered no romance, no adventure, and no outlet for his mind and body. The math classes were not sufficient stimulation, nor was his heavy schedule of job-related and educational priorities.

So he went to plays, read a lot, and worked on some short stories he had begun while he was a full-time student. In

Henry Irving at the time Bram first met him.

1872, he sold a short story "The Crystal Cup" to a magazine called *London Society*. He also continued to read Walt Whitman's works. Finally, he got up the nerve to write to Whitman. He wrote almost 2000 words including: "Put it [the letter] in your fire if you like, but if you do you will miss the pleasure of this next sentence." In contrast to this bragging, he adopted an inferior attitude: "You are a true man, and I would like to be one myself, and so I would be towards you as a brother and as a pupil to his master..."

Stoker described himself to the poet: "...I am ugly but strong and determined and have a large bump over my eyebrows. I have a heavy jaw and a big mouth and thick lips—sensitive nostrils—a snub nose and straight hair." He told Whitman that he was somewhat secretive, even-tempered, self-controlled.

But all this unburdening came to nothing. He put the letter in a desk drawer. Maybe he meant to take it out later and work on it some more. Maybe he thought the letter was useless since he could not expect to meet Whitman in person. Whatever his intention at the time, he did not mail the letter. Still, he continued to read and re-read his favorite poet's work and to collect autographed copies

As critic for the *Evening Mail*, he had tickets for opening nights, and he was allowed to spend time backstage with the cast. He continued to study plays in print before he attended performances. He learned about stage lighting and scenery, about casting and directing, and about the impact of dialogue and action scenes. He found friendly faces and interesting conversations among those who worked at the theater.

Like an evangelist, Stoker wanted to spread the good news about the wonderful happenings at the theater. Flushed with the excitement of an opening night play, he wrote his criticisms right after the curtain closed. But no matter how quickly he wrote he could not meet the deadline the editor imposed. His reviews never made the next day's paper. Stoker learned that his deadline included an allowance for trouble with the cumbersome pulleys and wheels that comprised the printing press. Stoker was able to persuade the editor to grant him an hour extension on the deadline. After that, his reviews came out the day after each performance.

Stoker wrote about more than performances. Sometimes he talked about the audience. Once he scolded newspaper readers for not attending a particular play, asking why they didn't appreciate intellectual drama. Another time he commented on the rowdy audience members who shouted during the play.

Stoker wrote to his family. He told them that he wanted to give up his civil service career and become a play writer.

He mentioned that he had a particular actress in mind for a major part. His father tried to persuade him to stay in the civil service which, he said, was a much more promising career than it had been earlier. Although Abraham, Sr. admitted that he enjoyed going to performances, he said that the theater did not have a good reputation. He told his son that it was best to stay away from the class of people who performed on the stage. He went on to say that actresses were little better than prostitutes and that actors were clowns, jesters, and men who would sell their souls for an audience.

His son saw an entirely different picture. But he was in no financial position to leave his steady wages at the Castle, and he made no move at that time.

In 1873, Stoker submitted a short story, "Jack Hammon's Vote," to three different magazines. Each time, it was rejected. When he sent it to a fourth magazine, he mentioned the previous three rejections in a cover letter: "I am anxious to see if you will add to the number." That fourth magazine also rejected the story.

The next year, he reached out again to Whitman. He wrote to him, telling him that his poems had helped him to be more open with people. He said that he would like to meet him personally. He also discussed the controversy about Whitman's work: "I wage a perpetual war with many

Abraham Stoker Sr. tried to warn his son away from a life in the theater.

friends on your behalf." This time, Stoker did not shove the letter into a desk drawer; he mailed it.

The poet wrote back: "You did well to write to me so unconventionally, so fresh, so manly, and so affectionately. I too hope (though it is not probable) that we shall one day meet."

An eligible bachelor, Stoker went to many parties and dinners. He was tall and graceful, a good dancer known for his waltzing. He made few friends at work, but sometimes went out to taverns with other writers. He lost track of some of his Trinity friends because they had different interests now—courting, marrying, professions, etc. He did keep contact with Oscar Wilde whom he had known at Trinity when he was a senior and Oscar was a freshman. Now Stoker sometimes dined with Oscar and his family. At the Wilde table, Stoker was delighted with the opportunity to talk about science, art, and literature with educated people.

Stoker was fascinated with Oscar's father and his tales of travels in Egypt. In one of his anecdotes, he told of finding a mummy that he took from the coffin and sent back to Ireland. He also told vampire tales including stories of *Dearg-due* who tempted men and then sucked their blood. He told of Irish fairies that kidnapped children to take their blood since the fairies had no blood of their own.

Oscar and Stoker shared their short story ideas with each

Bram enjoyed sharing stories with his classmate Oscar Wilde.

other. Because of his long childhood illness, Stoker had an advantage as a writer. Probably he had been told more short stories than most children had. Perhaps because he had spent so many lonely hours, he had learned to re-tell the stories to himself. And in his solitude, he had used his imagination to expand and exaggerate what he heard to deepen the mystery, drama, and suspense. Now he added to these memories his growing knowledge of dramatic arts. In one story, "Chain of Destiny," he used his experience at auditions to create a character called "the phantom of the fiend" who auditions for a role in a play.

In 1875, three of his stories were published in a popular weekly magazine, *The Shamrock*. They were published in serial form, one chapter at a time, in the publication. Serialization was popular, especially to the many readers who could not afford a hardcover book. Sometimes a single story would continue for a couple of years. One especially popular serial writer was Wilkie Collins whose novel *The Woman in White* featured a suspicious woman (was she really a ghost?), a mysterious disease, and a love triangle. This novel fit well into serial chapters because it was written in the form of dated journals written by different characters in the book.

Still studying for his degree at Trinity and working full time at Dublin Castle, Stoker found time to write unsigned editorials for a weekly paper. This newspaper, *The Warder*, championed the cause of Irish Protestants against Catholic pressures. He also took on an unpaid "job" for a new daily paper, the *Irish Echo*. There he wrote copy and sold advertising.

His father, who had earlier disapproved of Stoker's connections with the theater, now warned his son against connections with a newspaper. He warned the government did not approve of civil service workers with journalism connections. Stoker did not worry much about his reputation as a civil servant. He had no intention of staying on at Dublin Castle as long as his father had. In fact, he told his father, he planned to quit his job and move to London to write plays. Again, his father disapproved, warning Stoker that he would not be allowed to get back into government work if his drama career failed—as it probably would.

Stoker's father died in 1876. Abraham, Jr. went to Italy for the funeral and then returned to Dublin. Shortly after that, Stoker officially changed his first name to Bram.

This was the same year that Henry Irving returned to Dublin to star in *Hamlet*. This Shakespeare play appealed to Stoker for its air of mystery and scenes of madness. A central question of the play is "Are ghosts real?"

Stoker's review praised Irving's acting as Hamlet: "...Irving's physical appearance sets him at once above his fellows as no common man..." Still, he did not hesitate to show Irving's weaknesses: "...the voice lacks power to be strong in some tones, and in moments of passion the speech loses its clearness and becomes somewhat inarticulate."

Because Irving liked the review, he invited Stoker to dine with him at his hotel. The next night, they dined together again. That evening, Irving had a gift for Stoker and the other eleven guests—a recitation of the poem "The Dream of Eugene Aram," a story of eccentricity, murder, a corpse that will not stay buried, and a climax in which the murderer confesses and is hung. Stoker was so moved by the performance that, he said, "I became hysterical."

Chapter Three

Art and Business Meet

—AROUND THIS TIME—

Electric lights were installed on some London streets.
Alexander Graham Bell invented the telephone.
Gilbert and Sullivan wrote *H.M.S. Pinafore*.
Popular literature included:
The Adventures of Tom Sawyer by Mark Twain,
The American by Henry James,
The Return of the Native by Thomas Hardy.

Stoker courted Florence Balcombe whom he had known for many years. Stoker's friend Oscar Wilde also had courted Florence. Florence was outgoing and beautiful. Stoker said she was an "exquisitely pretty girl . . . just seventeen with the most perfectly beautiful face I ever saw."

Stoker was promoted to Inspector of Petty Sessions, a position that gave him a raise. It also required him to travel for weeks at a time to rural areas where there was no established court. An advantage of the job was that he watched hearings that gave him an excellent picture of rural Ireland. A disadvantage was that he missed many opening nights in Dublin, and he had to resign as drama critic.

Not content with simply recording the activities of the court, Stoker studied the judicial system. He kept notes for his own use, and he read documents about the court system dating back to 1851. Then he wrote a 248-page book, *The Duties of Clerks of Petty Sessions in Ireland*, in which he advocated court reform. Specifically, he suggested a uniform filing system and more efficient recording of collection and distribution of money. Later he described his book as a "complete guide to a clerk's daily duties, from how best to tot up accounts to how to collect fines, deal with dangerous idiots, debts, deserters, trespassing cattle and discovery of arms."

In a totally different tone and style, Stoker reviewed Irving's performance as Hamlet in 1877. This time he had nothing but praise for the actor: "... a wild, fitful, irresolute, mystic, melancholy prince that we know in the play; but given with a sad, picturesque gracefulness which is the actor's special gift."

While Irving was in Dublin, he, Stoker and other theater lovers frequently had dinner together in restaurants. Stoker spent a lot of time with Irving at rehearsals and performanc-

Oscar Wilde sketched this picture of Florence Balcombe in 1876.

es and also chatting with him in his dressing room.

In June, *Vanderdecken* opened starring Irving. This W. G. Wills play was based on the Flying Dutchman legend, the story of Captain Vanderdecken who defied God and therefore was doomed to sail until the Day of Judgement. After the opening, Stoker and Irving agreed that the play was too long. They worked together to shorten it. Stoker felt a deepening friendship: "We understood each other's nature, needs and ambitions, and had a mutual confidence, each towards the other in our own way, rare amongst men."

Soon after the performance of *Vanderdecken*, Irving became manager of the Lyceum, a 1500-seat theater in the middle of London's playhouse district. He sent Stoker a telegram: "Will you give up the Civil Service and join me, to take charge of my business as acting-manager?" Stoker accepted readily. He resigned his job. In December 1878, he and nineteen-year-old Florence were married in Dublin in a Protestant church. Right after the ceremony, they traveled to London. Stoker wanted to be on hand whenever summoned by Irving, the man whom he called the "chief" or "Guv'nor.

The Bram Stokers rented a top-floor flat near a busy market that sold produce, kitchen equipment, and other household supplies. In the dingy neighborhood, street gutters overflowed with sewage and garbage. Pedestrians scurried out of the way when carriages rumbled through the narrow streets. About 80,000 homeless people slept in unsanitary and unsafe shelters. Although some sewerpipes had been built, most wastewater flowed into the Thames River. Since the river was a source of drinking water, cholera outbreaks were frequent.

Stoker set a high goal for himself. He resolved to make the Lyceum the finest theater in London. Part of his plan was to pay actors so well that none would refuse his offer of a role. Another part of the plan was to redecorate the theater inside and out.

He faced a strict deadline. The first play in the new Lyceum would open just two weeks after his arrival in London. He worked intensely on renovation, decor, and staging. In his writing, Stoker had learned the importance of color, texture, and lighting in scenes. Now he used this sensory awareness to create a mood of elegance as he decorated the theater.

He had much more than decor on his mind. He also worked with ticketing, seating arrangements, and publicity. As a sickly child, he had lived with a ritual of meals and visits from family members. Now as theater manager, he made a ritual of creating and adhering to lists and schedules.

Even on opening night, he could not relax. In fact, his schedule was even more hectic on the first night of the play than it was in the hectic days of preparation. First, he checked the box office for last-minute messages, some of which demanded immediate attention. Then he examined all the carpets, drapes, and seats. He checked the orchestra pit for cleanliness and arrangement of chairs and music stands. He inspected the gaslights. Then he called the ushers to attention and gave them their orders.

As curtain call approached, women in long gowns and men in top hats stepped from their horse-drawn cabs into the newly decorated theater. When playgoers entered the foyer, they saw a dramatic scene. Gaslight candles shone on walls and ceilings of blue, green, and gold. Tall red-haired and red-bearded Stoker stood at the top of the staircase, dramatic in black and white formal dress. He personally welcomed each member of the audience. He bowed, smiled, and shook hands alike with those he knew and those he did not. His dramatic style made a strong statement about the future of the Lyceum in London.

After that opening play, Stoker jumped into the business of keeping the theater running.

Renovations had left Irving with a 12,000-pound debt. As acting manager, Stoker took on the responsibility of paying back the money and then creating a profit.

Much of his work involved writing letters. Postage for a letter was one penny a half-ounce, and mailmen delivered

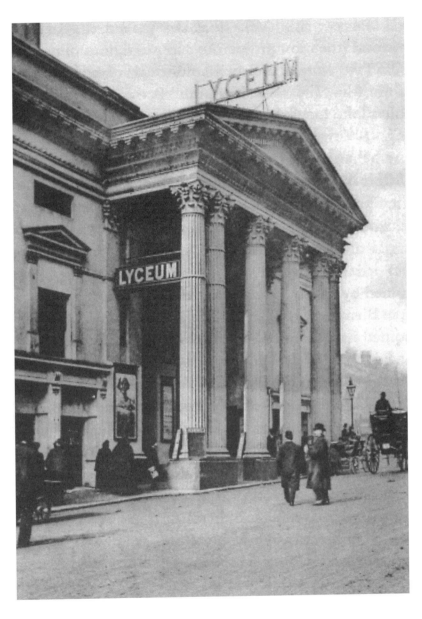

Bram was determined to make the Lyceum the finest theater in London.

two and three times a day. Stoker corresponded with actors, suppliers, potential crewmembers, benefactors, and members of the audience. He wrote as many as fifty letters a day and said about this correspondence: "Fortunately—for both myself and the readers, for I write an extremely bad hand—the bulk of them were short." Also fortunately for him, he had learned to write quickly and accurately in his work as a drama critic.

He spent time with stage builders, plasterers, painters, and upholsterers. He added innovations to theater management. He numbered expensive seats to avoid confusion and to encourage advance booking. In an effort to build attendance, he advertised performances.

Stoker renovated a suite for guests at the theater. He installed a modern kitchen range, brought crystal champagne glasses, and decorated the walls with armor and portraits. Often he and Irving invited guests to dine there after a performance. For these late night suppers, Stoker arranged place cards to insure seating that he considered appropriate. He also kept the conversation going, not allowing private conversations among guests. As a theater manager, he worked to provide the same kind of predictability and comfort for his guests that he had appreciated as a child who yearned for company.

A perfectionist in all aspects of play production, Stoker

studied in the British Library, then a part of the British Museum, to create authentic scenery and details.

He resented the fact that he was expected to take on so many tasks. Before moving to London, he had worked at two jobs and attended university at the same time. Now as Lyceum manager, he faced an even heavier schedule. Sometimes the strain of all the responsibility became too much for him. He became short tempered at times. To make matters worse, Irving was quick to criticize—and Stoker was slow to accept disapproval of his work. In turn, he criticized those who worked under him. With two Trinity degrees, Stoker was more educated than most of his fellow workers. This achievement may have given him a superior attitude, and this attitude may have aroused discomfort and unrest among those with whom he worked.

Stoker added another problem to his life with his belief that Irving should not be bothered with financial worries. To make sure that the star was completely shielded from such problems, Stoker kept all financial records hidden. No one in the management was allowed to see the ledgers, thus insuring that no information would be slipped to Irving even unintentionally.

Freed of financial concerns, Irving demanded lavish new sets, costumes, and props. He insisted on realism—real food in banquet scenes, real trees and flowers in scenery, real gold on crowns and other royal trappings.

Irving's career flourished under these conditions. In 1878, he played again in *Vanderdecken*. Again the audience thrilled to the profound question: "Where are we?" and the answer: "Between the living and the dead." Stoker was excited about Irving's performance. He wrote: "[Irving] gave one a wonderful impression of a dead man fictitiously alive." He continued: "[Irving's eyes] seemed to shine like cinders of glowing red from out the marble face."

Chapter Four

Travels Bring Successes and Trials

In late 1879, the Lyceum scheduled 250 consecutive performances of Shakespeare's *The Merchant of Venice*. Stoker believed that Irving's creation of the ruthless character Shylock was inspired. A reviewer agreed, calling the performance "...noble and sordid, pathetic and terrifying." After the first hundred extremely successful presentations of the play, Stoker celebrated with a huge party. He invited 350 prominent guests, set decorations all over the stage, gave out copies of the play on white parchment with gold lettering, and served a seven-course meal.

Florence gave birth to Irving Noel Thornley Stoker on December 31, 1879. Stoker was thrilled with his son, but little Irving added a complication to his life. Besides production duties, Stoker had assumed the responsibility of catering to Irving's every desire. The star believed that he needed Stoker's company each night after a performance. He said that he needed Stoker to help him to unwind and to release the tension built up on the stage.

Stoker never knew what tasks Irving might give him from day to day. When he was not at the theater, Irving often sent messages to Stoker, asking for help. Sometimes he simply seemed to need attention. Many messages were about insignificant matters: please do an errand for me; bring soup for my lunch; invite so-and-so to dine with us. On a typical day, Stoker left home late in the morning and stayed at the theater until sunrise. This schedule left little time for a baby, and Stoker could not easily change the relationship he had built up over the years with Irving. Perhaps he didn't want to.

Florence Stoker knew that she could not depend on her husband for either help or company. Her husband placed

The busy Bram spent little time at home with Florence and his son Noel.

Irving's needs as his first priority. So Florence took care of herself, making her own friends and social engagements, and enjoying life in London. When she became nervous, she took laudanum, a commonly used form of opium, to calm her nerves, as did many people of those times.

Stoker had once imagined that he might become an actor. In 1880, he took the part of an extra in a play about twin brothers with a supernatural bond. A rack of large cloaks, masks, and floppy hats stood ready for anyone connected with the play who wanted to be on stage for a masked ball scene. Stoker took part in a dance scene with clowns. Irving laughed at him, but Stoker was serious about his part. "I couldn't myself see anything of a mirthful nature," he commented, irritated with Irving's scorn.

That same year, Stoker again felt the urge to write. He took out the notes he had made and kept as a child—fairy tales, stories his mother had told him, and his notes about legends. He found plenty of material for new plots.

In one story, "The Invisible Giant," he recalled his mother's description of the cholera epidemic. The Giant in the story is a plague. A young girl and an elderly man are the only two characters aware of the coming of the Giant who will destroy evildoers. The old man ". . .knew that the Giant was a very terrible one; and his heart wept for the doomed city where so many would perish in the midst of their sin."

HOW JOHN JENKINS
WON HIS MEDAL

P.C. JOHN JENKINS

M.R BRAM STOKER

M.R BRAM STOKER'S
GALLANT ACT.

This newspaper illustration praises Bram for his rescue of a man who attempted to commit suicide by jumping in the Thames.

In "The Voice of the Great Present," Stoker has his main character, the Shadow Builder, create a special space where ". . .all things lose their being and become part of the great *Is-Not.* . . . Whosoever passes into it disappears. . . ."

His theme for these and six other stories was a common one in children's literature—good wins over evil. Stoker reinforced this theme with a warning: ". . .the things we do wrong . . . come back to us with bitterness. . . ." In 1882, thirty-five-year-old Stoker published this collection of eight fairy tales in his first full-length book, titled *Under the Sunset.* He dedicated the book to his son Noel.

The British humor magazine *Punch* called it "a charming book," and a *New York Tribune* reviewer said, ". . .the thoughts of the book are high and pure. . . ."

That was the year that Stoker became a hero. Usually, he began and ended his workday with a trip across the Thames on a ferry. These trips were generally uneventful, but on one September day, an elderly man jumped off the boat, trying to commit suicide. Stoker reached out to drag him back onto the boat but grasped only his jacket. In a flash, Stoker whisked off his coat and jumped into the river. He swam to the man, grabbed hold of him, and managed to keep him afloat until a boat appeared. For his quick and unselfish action, Stoker received a bronze medal from the Royal Humane Society.

It was back to the British Library for Stoker when the Lyceum contracted to do a play, *The Cup*, by Alfred Lord Tennyson, later poet laureate of England. At the library, Stoker studied in the reading room. There, like many other patrons, he had his own desk and chair and a peg to hang his hat on. He studied architecture and history so that he could instruct theater workers on construction of a temple of Artemis on the stage. He also helped designers to embroider costumes for the lead actress and supporting players. Reviewers praised the setting as an artistic triumph, although many considered the play as less than a dramatic triumph.

An interesting sidelight to his work on *The Cup* was Stoker's friendship with Tennyson. Tennyson was particularly pleased that Stoker could quote some of his poems from beginning to end.

Stoker's work became international in the 1880s. At that time, steamships carried passengers across the Atlantic in less than two weeks. British actors sometimes traveled to America to perform for audiences there, and American actors sometimes acted in British specials. In 1883, the Lyceum sent Irving, one of Irving's favorite actresses Ellen Terry, and an entire company to America for a six-month tour. Before the tour, Stoker set up a full schedule of publicity and public relations. He also took care of many personal responsibilities for Irving. He settled the actor's two young sons at school, visited Irving's relatives, and completed necessary correspondence. After saying good-bye to Irving who sailed on the *S.S.Brittanic*, Stoker took care of his own family by leaving them with Florence's mother in Dublin.

Then he set to work loading tons of equipment for twelve plays onto the *City of Rome*. The equipment included painted scenery, props, calcium lights, and costumes. He arranged schedules, gathered baggage, and fulfilled special requests for about a hundred performers and other people who worked in the theater. Finally, Stoker was on his way to New York. Besides all his wishes for the success of the performances, he had one more wish—he wanted to see Walt Whitman.

Once in New York, Stoker immediately immersed himself in the business details of the trip—overseeing hotel accommodations; transporting of props, costumes, and scenery; dealing with reporters, solving personnel problems, and settling conflicts for cast members and workers.

The company appeared first at the Star Theater in New York City in a highly praised performance of *The Bells.* Irving starred again as a man who was haunted by the murder he committed. The company also received high praise for *Hamlet*, which they played in Philadelphia. In a

The Lyceum produced Alfred Lloyd Tennyson 's play, *The Cup*.

highly dramatic scene, Irving as Hamlet threw a cup of poisoned wine onto the stage. The startled audience gasped. They thought they saw a flow of blood pouring from the cup. The illusion was cleverly created with red sawdust

Performances succeeded; travel arrangements did not. The American agent who scheduled the tour did not plan the route carefully. Sometimes the performers seemed to wait endlessly; at other times, they showed up late for appointments.

The company traveled to cities as widespread as Detroit and Baltimore, St. Louis and Toronto, Providence and Cincinnati. Stoker met the constant challenge of getting equipment and people on and off trains in all kinds of weather and conditions. It was impossible to avoid delay; train wheels cracked because of the cold, an engine exploded, railway tracks washed out in a flood; a train caught on fire, railway bridges collapsed.

On a happier note, the company received lots of invitations to dinners, social clubs, and other entertainments. Perhaps their most famous host was President Chester Arthur who invited them to dinner at the White House.

Stoker became a friend with writer Mark Twain. They found a mutual interest in their writing. In particular, they discussed the roles of nightmares and the subconscious in their stories.

Twain had another interest that he shared with both Irving and Stoker. He convinced them to invest in typesetter stock, telling them ". . . in three years I judge that this stock will bring fabulous prices. . ." Stoker bought twenty shares at $50 each, to be paid for on an installment plan.

Through all the work and excitement, Stoker's mind was on Walt Whitman. When would he meet the poet with whom he had corresponded? He had hoped to meet him in Philadelphia but simply could not find time. He sent a note to the writer: ". . . If I ever do it [meet you] it will be one of the greatest pleasures in my life."

Another goal for Stoker was to find out everything he could about America. He bought copies of congressional reports, history books, studies of the Constitution, schoolbooks, and etiquette books. He went out of his way to speak to Americans in many different occupations quizzing them about their lives and work.

Chapter Five

Realism Demands Research

—AROUND THIS TIME—

More females worked as domestic servants than in any other job.
Some transatlantic ships used propellers instead of paddle wheels.
The first skyscraper, 10 stories high, was built in Chicago.
Popular literature included:
Treasure Island by Robert Louis Stevenson,
The Arabian Nights by Richard Burton,
A Study in Scarlet by Sir Arthur Conan Doyle.

Finally, on a trip to America in 1884, Stoker met Whitman. The men chatted about their correspondence, their writing, and many other aspects of their lives. They had a wonderful time. Stoker described Whitman: ". . .great shaggy masses of grey-white hair fell over his collar. His moustache was large and thick and fell over his mouth so as to mingle with the top of the mass of the bushy flowing beard." In turn, Whitman described Stoker as: ". . .a breath of good, healthy, breezy sea air." He said that Stoker treated him as a favorite son would treat him.

That meeting changed Stoker's life. He decided that now, at age forty, he should make writing a priority in his life. Nine years as stage manager for the Lyceum had shown him that theater work demanded his complete attention. He could not work for the Lyceum and pursue a writing career at the same time. Still, a writing career would not meet his financial needs. What other career would allow him some flexibility in scheduling so that he could write? He decided on law. He believed that he would be able to schedule a law practice to allow time for writing.

Law classes were available, but he did not have to attend regularly. To be accepted as a lawyer, he had only to eat in the student hall once during each of twelve terms and to pass written and oral examinations. Concepts of law were not completely new to Stoker. He had learned about court processes while working at Dublin Castle. He dug even deeper in his research for *Petty Sessions*. So Stoker did not attend any classes. However, he did study often in the library. There he used a special room called the Inner Temple. Sometimes he could not resist working on his fiction, instead of law, in this room. Despite his heavy schedule, he began work on a novel and some short stories.

When friends asked why he chose law, Stoker joked that

he did it avoid jury duty because lawyers are not asked to sit on juries. Perhaps the real reason was to build his own career instead of working to expand Irving's career.

In 1886, he gathered together the notes he had taken in America. These became a lecture, "A Glimpse of America," which he presented in London and also as a pamphlet. Stoker included fascinating trivia like the fact that America had over 124,000 miles of railroad and that more than 11,000 newspapers and periodicals were published in the country. He criticized the ignorance of Britons about America: ". . .[it is] deplorable that we can be left so ignorant of a nation . . .with whom our manifold interests are not only vast, but almost vital..." Stoker ended with a plea for mutual understanding: "...we are bound each to each by the instinct of a common race..." Both his lecture and his pamphlet were well received. Stoker, a behind-the-scenes worker for seven years, now received some applause himself.

Stoker learned a lot about scenes, descriptions, costumes, and dialogue when he worked with Irving in *Faust*, a long poem by the German writer Goethe that became a play. Irving played the part of Mephistopheles, the devil. Faust is a character who sells his soul to Mephistopheles in return for magic power and eternal youth. Doing research for this production, Stoker and Irving and other members of the company walked around Nuremberg, Germany to study

Walt Whitman as he looked when Bram met him in 1884.

buildings and terrain to serve as backdrop to Goethe's scenes. They investigated Nuremberg's old castle and the torture tower. In that tower, they found an Iron Virgin, a cabinet lined with spikes into which a condemned criminal was placed.

In one scene of the play, Mephistopheles appeared from a cleft in the rocks. Lightning flashed, thunder roared, and the air was filled with inhuman sounds. Witches flew across the stage on broomsticks, and 250 warlocks, demons, imps, and goblins pranced and danced on the stage, screeching, howling, and banging.

Stoker was particularly proud of the use of electricity in this play. He wrote: "twenty years ago electric energy, in its playful aspect, was in its infancy. . . . [in this play] two iron plates were screwed upon the stage at a given distance so that at the time of fighting each of the swordsmen would have his right boot on one of the plates . . . a wire was passed up the clothing of each from the shoe to the outside of the India rubber glove, in the palm of which was a piece of steel. Thus when each held his sword a flash came whenever the swords crossed." Limelight, made by heating lime (calcium oxide) on an oxyhydrogen flame, was used to good advantage. The light was extremely bright, especially good for pointing to a spot, creating sunrises and sunsets, and highlighting an aspect of the scene.

Bram Stoker in 1884.

Stoker also used research when he wrote "The Squaw," a story about a satanic cat. At the end, as the hero dies, impaled on spikes in a door, the narrator says: "And sitting on the head of the poor American was the cat, purring loudly as she licked the blood which trickled through the gashed sockets of his eyes. I think no one will call me cruel because I seized one of the old executioners' swords and shore her in two as she sat."

In the fall of 1886, Stoker went to America to make arrangements to show *Faust* in that country. He asked Florence to come with him on the trip. She declined, saying that the trip would be too long and difficult for Noel.

Stoker again visited Walt Whitman in Philadelphia. Although Whitman was not well, he welcomed Stoker. They spent an hour together talking mostly about Abraham Lincoln, appreciating their mutual admiration for the President. Stoker took back to England with him Whitman's' *Memoranda During the War* which described, among other things, Lincoln's assassination. Stoker's list of personal heroes expanded—Irving, Whitman, and now Lincoln.

Stoker's writing career grew and flourished. In "The Duelists: or, the Death Doom of the Double Born," published in 1887, two young boys, Harry and Tommy, cut up lots of items including carpets and cats. They also hack at the faces of toddler twins. Panicked, their father raises a gun and shoots. In the end, "...As the smoke cleared off Ephraim [the father]. . . saw Harry and Tommy, all unhurt, waving in the air the trunks of the twins—the fond father had blown the heads completely off his own offspring."

In April 1887, Florence and Noel survived a disastrous shipwreck. They were adrift for twelve hours before a tugboat rescued them. Still, Florence agreed to go to America with Stoker on the Lyceum tour that year. Aboard the ship, husband and wife experienced different emotions. Stoker loved a violent crossing. He found excitement and drama in the energy of the sea. He kept notes of the experience: ". . .[clouds] so dank and damp and cold that it needed but little effort of imagination to think that the spirits of those lost at sea were touching their living brethren with the clammy hands of death. . ." In sharp contrast, Florence was frantic with fear throughout the trip.

When he was not busy with his wife and son on the voyage, Stoker worked on a lecture about Lincoln, using some of Whitman's work as resource. He promised himself to give a lecture on Lincoln in America.

Once on land, Florence's health and spirits returned. Stoker enjoyed showing her and Noel the sights he was now familiar with.

Stoker kept his promise about his Lincoln research. He presented his Lincoln lecture in New York at Chickering

Hall on November 25, 1887. A reviewer said that the talk might have been fine for "ignorant" British, but it fell flat for Americans.

When he visited Whitman the following month, Stoker tried to convince the poet to edit out some of *Leaves of Grass* so that it would be more acceptable to Victorian society. He begged Whitman to let his friends help with the cutting: ". . .about a hundred lines in all—your books will go into every house in America. Is not that worth the sacrifice?" Absolutely not, answered Whitman: ". . .I think that all that God made is for good—and that the work of His hands is clean in all ways if used as He intended! No, I shall never cut a line so long as I live!"

Chapter Six

Writing Competes with the Theater

—AROUND THIS TIME—

A cheap box camera was introduced.
The first performance of Tchaikovsky's
Swan Lake was given.
Annual Nobel Prizes were established.
Popular literature included:
The Happy Prince and Other Tales by Oscar Wilde,
The Jungle Book by Rudyard Kipling,
The Time Machine by H. G. Wells.

In March, the Lyceum cast and crew performed at West Point Naval Academy for the cadets and officers there. The academy hall used for performances was too small to contain the usual complement of scenery for *The Merchant of Venice*. Stoker had the crew use Shakespeare's technique for scenery. On the curtain, they fastened labels designating buildings and locations: "Venice: a Public Place"; "Belmont:

Portia's House"; "Shylock's House by a Bridge." The audience loved the performance.

Back in England in 1888, Stoker gave his Lincoln lecture, "Abraham Lincoln: How the Statesman of the People Saved the Union, and Abolished Slavery in the Civil War." It was well received. In the talk, he discussed abstract ideas like the relationship of slaves and masters (he was against slavery). He also recited specific details including the size of Lincoln's feet and the color of his eyes.

Stoker knew America well. In eight tours—four years— the Lyceum traveled by train from New York City to San Francisco, from New Orleans to Montreal, and to and from dozens of cities in between.

Fires intrigued Stoker. Those who worked at the Lyceum noted his curiosity whenever the fire bell rang. Once when a curtain ignited during a play, Stoker grabbed a fleeing member of the audience. "Go back to your seat, sir," he shouted. "It is cowards like you who cause death to helpless women."

He was also intrigued with morgues. When he and Irving visited Paris, they enjoyed a special pastime. The city morgue was open to the public, and the two men visited often. There they stared at the victims and made up tales to account for the facial expressions. They also went to criminal courts to watch faces of the accused.

In 1888, the Lyceum prepared to stage Shakespeare's *Macbeth*, a play of murder, guilt, and ghosts. The play centers on a lonely castle, so Stoker, Irving, and other members of the company toured the castles of Scotland, noting architectural details that would bring reality to the scenes. On his trip, Stoker visited Cruden Bay, a fishing village near Aberdeen on the North Sea. He stayed at an inn called the Kilmarnock Arms and spent his days hiking over cliffs and dunes, enjoying the solitude, wild rabbits, grasses, and flowers. He wandered through the pink granite ruins of Slain's Castle, a 300-year-old structure. He enjoyed the peaceful view of the small fishermen's cottages, and the fishing nets stretched on high poles like a line of black tents. Attracted to the isolation of the bay, he determined to re-visit it at some time.

The Lyceum production of *Macbeth* was well received. Right from the opening scene of witches casting a spell— "When shall we three meet again/ In thunder, lightning, or in rain?"—the audience was captivated. They remained spellbound through the unfolding of the plot with its super-natural tone and its scenes of murder, suicide, and spiritual torment.

Like *Faust*, *Macbeth* appealed to the nineteenth century interest in the occult. This was an era of seances, clairvoy-ance, palm reading, and crystal ball gazing. Stoker shared these interests, and he explored them in his theater work. He said: "I often say to myself that the faith which still exists is to be found more often in a theatre than in a church."

Interest in the occult led Stoker to *The Land Beyond the Forest: Facts, Figures, and Fancies from Transylvania* by Emily Gerard, the wife of an Austrian soldier stationed in Romania. In this book, Gerard wrote about the beauty of the landscape, the "indolent charm and the drowsy poetry", and the "strange and incongruous companions" she had met there. She described ages-old stories of ogres, giants, and sorcerers as dramatized by storytellers called *provestitore*. She included a lot of material about superstitions revolving around devils, witches, dragons, and vampires. She also wrote about former humans whose penance for their sins was transformation into werewolves who attacked people.

Stoker became fascinated with Gerard's stories of Romanian customs of death and dying. Gerard wrote that each Romanian peasant made his own coffin long before he needed it. Part of the construction process included fitting himself into the burial box to test its size and strength. Family members were instructed to prepare a special pillow for the coffin because even a small imperfection would prevent the body from resting in its grave.

Stoker also learned more about nosferatu, vampires, from this book. He learned Gerard's "recipes" for getting

Ellen Terry, one of the most famous actresses of her time, spent most of her career with Stoker and Irving at the Lyceum.

rid of vampires: driving a stake through the corpse or shooting into the coffin. Gerard added: "In very obstinate cases of vampirism it is recommended to cut off the head, and replace it in the coffin with the mouth filled with garlic..."

Stoker and Hall Caine, another fiction writer, explored their mutual interests in spiritualism and in writing. Caine was six years younger than Stoker, and the author of *The Eternal City*, a novel so popular that it sold a million copies. Hall frequently wrote about subjects like sin and guilt, evil, spiritual degradation, romance, and revenge.

Caine was like Stoker in several ways. He too was meticulous about research for his novels. In an interview, he told a reporter that he had studied hundreds of volumes in connection with the writing of *The Eternal City*. He too had a family history of storytelling, and he and Stoker sat up night after night telling tales of ghosts and other supernatural beings. Caine was also fascinated with theater in general and with Irving in particular.

Stoker and his family vacationed in Whitby in 1890. This was a small town of fishermen on the coast of the North Sea in northern England. Stoker spent time exploring and savoring the atmosphere of the town and coastline. Everywhere he went, Stoker made notes—talking to fishermen, studying tombstones in the cemetery, listening to local tales like one favorite about an "undead" man. He studied logbooks and weather manuals, and he talked to residents about winds, clouds, and other signs of weather changes.

As in his childhood, Stoker was fascinated with life near the sea. He climbed the 199 steps to St. Mary's Church and graveyard, a high point from which he admired the North Sea in all its personalities. He spent a lot of time with sailors, enchanted with their tales of shipwrecks and drowns. He showed particular interest in the shipwreck of the Russian vessel *Dmitry* that occurred that year, and he pored over newspaper accounts in local newspapers. An intriguing aspect of the story was that the cargo on the ship was sand brought from the Danube delta.

In Whitby, Stoker visited the library often. He fed his fascination for Transylvania with *An Account of the Principalities of Wallachia and Moldavia* by William Wilkinson. He made notes about the land and customs of Romania, using books and maps from the library. He included notes about the Romanian language like: "Dracula in Wallachian (Wallach is a province in Romania) means devil." He searched for information on the Carpathian Mountains, an important European mountain system that ranges through Romania. A sample of his notes: "Carpathian roads almost impossible in winter, mud, and great stones rolled down on brink of precipice. . ."

He read books about superstitions and legends, books with titles like *Curious Myths of the Middle Ages, The Book of Were-Wolves, The Origin of Primitive Superstitions*, and *History of the Devil.* His notes about superstitions include: "...the *penangulan* takes possession of the forms of women, turns them into witches, and compels them to . . . fly by night to gratify a vampire craving for human blood. . .". He made a note that ". . .Night before Easter Sunday witches and demons are abroad and hidden treasures then flower. . ."

He learned some common Romanian beliefs about death and burial: death is only a sleep; mourners make holes in the coffin so the dead can hear. Stoker also held conversations and wrote lengthy letters to Hungarian scholars who added details of folklore, language, and idioms, and other aspects of local color.

He was fascinated with a fifteenth-century Romanian tyrant known by several names: Vlad Dracula, Vlad Tepes, and Vlad the Impaler. Among the stories told and re-told about Vlad is one that pictures him eating his lunch in a garden. Around him are the bodies of lawbreakers impaled on stakes as punishment for their crimes. Part of the story is that Vlad particularly enjoyed watching his victims' blood drain away.

Stoker also made notes about his daily life, jotting down his thoughts on any available scrap of paper—an envelope,

Vlad Dracula, who was also called Vlad the Impaler because he enjoyed impaling his subjects on stakes, was one of the models for Dracula.

a piece of stationery, a menu. He wrote of a dinner partner: "I sat next to him at supper, and the idea that he was dead was strong on me. I think he had taken some mighty dose of opium, for he moved and spoke like a man in a dream. His eyes, staring out of his white waxen face, seemed hardly the eyes of the living." In another note, he said that another acquaintance looked more dead than alive. In yet another note, Stoker described a friend's laughing face: ". . .[his] upper lip rose and his canine tooth showed its full length like the gleam of a dagger."

Stoker was intrigued with a new acquaintance, Dr. Arminius Vambery, a professor at the University of Budapest. Vambery was an expert in folklore with a particularly strong interest in the supernatural. He and Stoker talked often about eastern European superstitions in places like Transylvania, a section of Romania.

While collecting his notes, Stoker also worked on two novels. The first was *The Snake's Pass*. He called this his "outdoor" book because he wrote a lot of it outside during August vacations in any spare hour. He also worked on it whenever he found a free moment on his American tour.

The scene is the Irish coast, and the main character, like Stoker, feels an almost mystical connection to the sea. This suspenseful story involves a disembodied voice, old superstitions, and buried treasure. Like some of his earlier stories,

Vlad Dracula stayed at this castle in present day Romania.

The Snake's Pass was published in serial form in the magazine *The People* and in some newspapers. The book was immediately popular.

He also worked on a novel titled *Miss Betty* that he dedicated to his wife. Miss Betty is a sweet and beautiful young woman who falls in love with a handsome young man who tries to manipulate her money from her. In the book, Stoker included some gruesome touches in a description of Miss Betty: "The red glare of the sunset fell full upon her, smiting her pale face and snowy garments till from head to foot she looked as if dipped in blood." Reliving his rescue of the elderly man in the Thames, he included a rescue scene on that same river. Unsatisfied with the manuscript, Stoker did not publish this book immediately.

Probably his training in journalism enabled him to write so much and so quickly. His theater work undoubtedly helped him to learn realistic dialogue. During play rehearsals, actors and actresses sometimes asked Stoker to change their lines to make them sound more appropriate to the character. One of the most famous actresses, Ellen Terry, might say, "I would like something to convey the idea of _____." She would complete her thought; Stoker then rewrote the lines; the rehearsals continued.

Chapter Seven

Count Dracula Casts His Spell

—*AROUND THIS TIME*—

Katzenjammer Kids, the first comic strip, was created in America.
The British celebrated Queen Victoria's Diamond Jubilee.
The first modern Olympics were held in Athens, Greece.
Popular literature included:
Poems by W. B. Yeats,
The Sea Gull by Anton Chekhov,
Cyrano de Bergerac by Edmond Rostand.

In 1890, Stoker was admitted to the bar after four fairly easy years of study. But now he was deep into writing projects, and he felt no desire to pursue his earlier plans of becoming a lawyer.

In 1891, Stoker took out the *Miss Betty* manuscript again. He asked Hall Caine for his opinion. Caine told him that he believed the story was too flat and predictable. Again, Stoker put the manuscript away.

Stoker did not have time or energy to become frustrated with writing disappointments. His theater responsibilities still demanded considerable attention. He would not let his writing take priority over his duties to Irving and to the Lyceum. He continued to insist on the highest possible degree of realism in staging. For an 1892 run of Shakespeare's *Henry VIII*, he sent assistants to a museum to make drawings of tapestry, architecture, jewelry, costumes, and other physical details of the early sixteenth century when Henry ruled. Then Stoker and others pored over the drawings, made models, and finally created the stage settings which helped to make *Henry VIII* such a success that it ran for 203 performances.

For all Stoker's seriousness about his work, he found a lot of humor in it. He told of an actor who was supposed to say "Cool it with a Dragoon's blood," but somehow the words "baboon's blood" kept coming out in rehearsals. In his nervousness during a performance, the actor again misspoke. He could not control his reaction: "... cool it with dragoon's blood—No, no, baboon's. My God! I've said it again! baboon's blood."

Stoker told of another actor whose lines included mention of God's "dwelling place". Stoker reported that the confused performer recited: "All shall be well in the immortal land where God hath His—Ah—um—His—apartments."

He clipped articles about reporters who wrote about the Lyceum. In one of these clippings, a newsman reported about Stoker that ". . . [his] duties are to see that there is mustard in the sandwiches and to take the dogs out for a run." He also clipped an article about a reporter who believed that he had a scoop when he spotted red gas tanks outside the theater. The writer assumed that these were oxygen tanks used by Irving, and that they indicated that Irving was a dying man. He rushed to get the news into print. After the article came out, the reporter discovered that the tanks held components necessary for creating limelight.

Even when it seemed that all of Stoker's energies were focused on Irving and the Lyceum, part of his mind remained with the notes he had made in Whitby. Just as he was insatiable in his search for details for his plays, so was he insatiable in his note taking for background information for his writing project. He continued to jot down ideas for his project on any available piece of paper—hotel stationery, account book pages, old letters.

He decided to set many scenes in Styria, a region in Austria. When he found time, he reviewed his notes and outlined the mood and events in scenes that came to him in flashes. He recorded some of these in complete sentences; he noted others in short phrases: ". . . the journey—wolves howl and surround—blue flames—driver stops—knife thrown and strange sounds." He gave some characters roles before he gave them names. He created a lawyer's clerk, a mad doctor, a mad patient, and a girl who will die in the story. Some of his notes were about health problems of his characters. He consulted with his brother Thornley, then a surgeon, asking him about injuries that cause coma or are fatal.

In 1893, he received an offer of another job. J. McNeill Whistler, later famous for his painting *Whistler's Mother*, asked Stoker to handle his financial affairs for him: "I really think it would be worth a good man's while . . . I would give half of all I earned to such a man." he said. Stoker refused the offer, probably because he did not want to make a commitment that might prevent him for answering Irving's every call. Also, his long term writing project was ever on his mind.

Stoker took a short vacation at Cruden Bay where he had studied so much about Romania. With part of his mind still on his unfinished project, he wrote a new story, "The Watter's Mou" (The Water's Mouth), focusing on places and people he met in Cruden. The story is a tragedy involving smuggling. He showed his awe of the sea when his main character, a boatman, saw "a mass that in the gloom of the evening and the storm looked like a tangle of wreckage—spar and sail and rope—twirling in the rushing water round a dead woman, whose white face was set in an aureole of floating hair."

Stoker sent his *Miss Betty* manuscript to a publisher. The editor rejected the manuscript saying that there was not enough plot. Forty-seven-year-old Stoker wanted to be a writer, but he had to admit that he could not make a living with his writing. And he needed to do more than make a living; he had to put away money for Noel's education.

Stoker and Irving continued to solve problems at the Lyceum almost as fast as they arose. For Cervantes' play *Don Quixote*, Stoker ordered a broken down old nag for Irving to ride as Quixote. The day of the performance, Stoker left the theater to get the nag. He came back empty-handed. The horse's owner had been fined for cruelty to animals, and the starving horse had been shot. Immediately, Irving and Stoker ordered a hansom-cab horse to take its place. That night, and every other opening night, they had the horse painted to simulate hollow bones and prominent ribs.

The Lyceum performed *Madame Sans-Gene*, a play about a father who severely mistreats his son. Stoker believed the play was realistic: "The history of the time lent itself to horrors," he said. But when a tortured body appeared on stage, bloody and beaten, some of the audience left. For the next night's performance, Stoker cut out that scene and some others that had disturbed the audience. But the word went out that the play was gruesome and disturbing. After a month of poor ticket sales, Stoker closed the play. This closing in response to audience disapproval was probably a good public relations move for the Lyceum. But financially, it added to the growing money problems of the theater. In a desperate attempt to save money, the usually extravagant Irving persuaded Stoker to reduce the insurance coverage on the property.

Stoker continued to work on his writing project. He gave names to his characters. The lawyer's clerk became Jonathan Harker; the mad doctor was Dr. Seward; the mad patient, Renfield; the girl who died, Lucy Westenra. At one point, he named his villain Count Wampyr, a Slavic spelling of *vampyr* and the foundation for our present word *vampire*. Then he changed the name from Count Wampyr to Count Dracula. Sometimes in his notes, he called him simply Drac. He changed the location of main scenes from Styria to Transylvania, Romania. His notes looked increasingly like the outline for a book. He filled in names and sketched in scenes noting the dates, and sometimes the times, of each action. He made brief but specific notations: "Aug. 11. bat outside Lucy's window"; "July 4. Jonathan at hospital."

Perhaps borrowing from Collins and his popular *The Woman in White*, Stoker decided to write his book almost

Books III. Chapters 27

29/7/92.

I
- ✓ 1 — Purchase of Estate. Harker & Mina
- ✓ 2 — Harker's Diary — Munich
- ✓ 3 — do munich (Bistritz – Borgo Pass. Castle)
- 4 — do Santes Vogl: Belongs to me
- 5 — Dr Seward's Diary — flyman.
- 6 — Lucy's letters. Seward. Texan
- 7 — Harkers Diary. escape. graveyard. London
- 8 — whitby. churchyard in cliff. owners re
- 9 — do . Storm. ship arrives. derelict

II
- 1 — Lucy finds. brooch. red gs in sunset
- 2 — Sleepwalking. the aroused. mina married
- 3 — Seward's Diary. Lucy in London. Dracula ill
- 4 — Wolf found. medical impasse. death of Lucy
- 5 — opening vault & suspects of Prof. the Vow
- 6 — Harker's Diary. mina on the track
- 7 — Searches. discoveries. Prof re Vampires, Texan
- 8 — Texan's diary — Transylvania
- 9 — Secret search. Counts house. Bloodied room.

III
- 1 — Return of Count
- 2 — Texan returns. Harker recognize. mina man
- 3 — Vigilance Committee. neckties party
- 4 — flaws & proofs
- 5 — The Count feeling helped in
- 6 — choice of dwellings.
- 7 — Displeasure of Count
- 8 — filing the documents the decision
- 9 — a tourist tale. S. flyman & Texan and —

In these notes for *Dracula*, Bram divided the chapters into sections with a short explanation of the action in each chapter.

completely in the form of letters and diaries. A typical journal entry shows Harker's confusion when he discovers that the Count has no reflection. Harker has been looking into his mirror while shaving: Suddenly I felt a hand on my shoulder, and heard the Count's voice saying to me, "Good morning." I started, for it amazed me that I had not seen him, since the reflection of the glass covered the whole room behind me . . . I turned to the glass again to see how I had been mistaken . . . there was no reflection of him in the mirror.

In a typical diary entry, Dr. Seward records his observation of Renfield, his mental patient: "He disgusted me much while with him, for when a horrid blow-fly, bloated with some carrion food, buzzed into the room, he caught it, held it exultantly for a few moments between his finger and thumb, and, before I knew what he was going to do, put it in his mouth and ate it. He argued quietly that it was very good and very wholesome."

In a letter to her best friend Lucy, Mina writes about seeing Harker, her fiancé, for the first time since he left Transylvania: "I found my dear one, oh, so thin and pale and weak-looking. All the resolution has gone out of his dear eyes. He is only a wreck of himself and he does not remember anything that has happened to him for a long time past."

The only exception to the letter and journal style is the speech of the count. In scenes where Count Dracula speaks, Stoker writes in dialogue: "You may go anywhere you wish in the castle, except where the doors are locked, where of course you will not wish to go. There is reason that all things are as they are."

The plot revolves around real estate agent Jonathan Harker who is sent to Transylvania to complete a sale of land to a Count. This count is Dracula, a vampire who wants to extend his blood-sucking operations to England. The plot includes vampire attacks, opening of graves, chase scenes on land and sea, and romance.

As a finishing touch, Stoker dedicated the book to Hall Caine, calling him Hommy-Beg, a loving nickname given to Caine by his grandmother. Stoker had spent more than seven years on this book, and he believed it was ready for publication.

Chapter Eight

A Writing Career Flourishes

—AROUND THIS TIME—

Ragtime music was popular in the United States.
The first Tour de France took place.
Speed limit for cars in Britain was 20 miles an hour.
Popular literature included:
The War of the Worlds by H. G. Wells,
Peter Rabbit by Beatrix Potter,
The Importance of Being Ernest by Oscar Wilde.

On May 18, 1897, around 9:30 in the morning, posters went up outside the Lyceum. They announced that Stoker would read his latest work, a manuscript to be titled either *Dracula* or *The Undead.* Such reading of a yet-to-be-published manuscript was not unusual. The oral presentation became an official request for copyright on the material. Fifteen Lyceum company actors took various parts for the four-hour reading. A small audience of crewmembers, performers, and a few passers-by listened. Some stayed for the whole performance; others came and went as they wanted or needed to.

Stoker's dream was to produce the story as a play with Henry Irving as Dracula. The first half of his dream could have come true. A reader from the Lord Chamberlain's office declared that the manuscript was morally fit to be performed on stage, and he granted it License #162. However, the second half of his dream shattered when Stoker asked Irving what he thought of the manuscript. Irving answered with just one word—"Dreadful!"

Two days after the reading, Stoker decided on the title. He chose *Dracula*.

On May 26 Stoker was at the bookstore when the first copies arrived. He had imagined that the published book might wear a red jacket with gilt letters highlighting his name and that of Dracula. The books were not bright red, and there was no gold on the cover at all. Instead, the novel was wrapped in a cheap yellow cloth cover, and the red letters *Dracula* by Bram Stoker hardly caught the eye. Despondent, Stoker wondered how many of the 3000 published copies would sell.

To relieve his disappointment, Stoker had boxed leather-bound copies made for his important friends, such as British Prime Minister William Gladstone, who was determined to rescue Ireland from centuries of British domination. He and Stoker had established a friendship in part because of their mutual support for an independent Ireland. With Gladstone's gift copy, Stoker sent a note: "the book is necessarily full of horrors and terrors, but I trust these are calculated to cleanse the mind by pity and terror."

His mother sent a "review": "My dear, it is splendid." Ignoring, or pretending to ignore, his father's research, Noel said that the plot for *Dracula* came to his father "in a nightmarish dream after eating too much dressed crab."

Reviewers offered differing opinions. *The Athenaeum* said the book ". . . reads at times like a mere series of grotesquely incredible events." A reviewer for the *Pall Mall Gazette* wrote: "It is excellent. One of the best things in the supernatural line." The *Daily Mail* called it a "weird, powerful and horrible story." Some reviewers noted with pleasure Stoker's introduction of modern inventions—the Kodak camera, the portable typewriter, the recording phonograph—into the book. One reviewer asked how Stoker dared to describe Romania since he had never been there. Stoker answered: "Trees are trees, mountains, are, generally speaking, mountains, no matter in what country you find them, and one description may be made to answer for all."

The book was not an instant success, but it sold steadily and well.

This cover is from a 1901 edition of *Dracula*.

Stoker finished *Miss Betty* and then worked on some stories with the Cruden Bay background.

In February 1898, a fire broke out in the storage area of the Lyceum. Costumes, scenery, and other stage properties for forty-four plays went up in flames. Irving and Stoker paid dearly for reducing their fire insurance in a money saving measure earlier. Stoker found himself with two heavy responsibilities. One was to recover whatever was salvageable and to create new props and scenery as necessary for the immediate future. The other was to reassure Lyceum patrons that the theater would soon re-open in all its splendor.

Stoker was hard at work on these tasks a few months later when Irving came down with pleurisy and pneumonia, both illnesses requiring a couple of month's rest. While he was still ill, Joe Comyns Carr, a leader in the cultural circles of England, visited the actor. Carr outlined a plan whereby a syndicate would take over the Lyceum.

Depressed and ill, Irving agreed on the spot. Under the conditions of the takeover, Irving would continue as actor-manager of the theater, would give one hundred performances each year, and would receive a cash settlement.

Stoker first heard of the agreement as he boarded a ship to America for the next Lyceum tour. He was hurt and angry that Irving had not consulted him. However, he carried on with his Lyceum commitments as though nothing had happened.

Meanwhile, sales of *Dracula* continued, so many that Stoker was invited to write a sketch about himself for *Who's Who*. In filling out the form for the entry, he found a blank after the word Recreations. He filled in "pretty much the same as the other children of Adam."

That year, Mark Twain came to London with an offer for Stoker. Twain's venture in typesetting stocks had failed, and he had returned Stoker's money. Now he had a new idea.

Twain wanted Stoker to act as agent for him in selling an adaptation of a German play. Although this idea did not work out, the two men renewed their friendship and their discussions of dreams, the sub-conscious, and dual personalities.

That same year, he found a publisher for *Miss Betty*. The reviews were good.

Stoker settled down to writing short stories. After seven long years of living with the challenge of *Dracula*, short-term projects sounded inviting. He found that he could write more or less when he wanted to—just a sentence here and there at times, and pages and pages when he was more inspired and had more time.

Some of his stories were particularly grim. In "The Squaw," Stoker described the details of a Torture Tower including swords used specifically for beheading, chairs full of nails, and the dreaded Iron Virgin torture device he had studied in Nuremberg. In "The Burial of the Rats," the narrator is forced to flee through the slums of Paris: "Splash! My feet had given way in a mass of slimy rubbish, and I had fallen headlong into a reeking, stagnant pool. The water and the mud in which my arms sank up to the elbows was filthy and nauseous beyond description, and in the suddenness of my fall I had actually swallowed some of the filthy stuff."

Good news for his writing career arrived when Doubleday & McClure announced the first American edition of *Dracula*. The story would also be serialized in newspapers in the States.

That same year, Stoker took his sixth trip to America for the Lyceum. Some of the most violent weather he had ever seen thrilled Stoker. He gloried in a hundred mile an hour hurricane, a strange storm without any rain. He stood at the rail, marveling at the mountainous waves and the wind roaring like a banshee, ". . . at times we rolled so that our feet shot off the deck." Trunks fastened to the deck strained at their ropes until they broke away. Stoker gashed his leg trying to catch and re-fasten them.

On that trip, Stoker received much more than usual attention. He was no longer simply Irving's valet. He stood on his own record as author of the much talked about *Dracula.* One reviewer seemed surprised that the writer of the latest horror novel was: ". . . a great shambling, good-natured overgrown boy . . . with a red beard, untrimmed, and a ruddy complexion tempered somewhat by the wide-open full grey eyes that gaze so frankly into yours."

Back in England, London was becoming a world center. City dwellers entered a new age with new and efficient sewers and water pipes, large stores, a subway, a telegraph cable, higher standards of living for workers, and a flurry of new magazines and newspapers. Competition among theaters increased. Back in 1878, the Lyceum was one of just seven city playhouses performing drama. By 1900, there were more than twice as many rivals for the attention of theatergoers. The city of London issued new safety regulations for public buildings. Some of these regulations would require expensive repairs and equipment. The Lyceum company decided to sell the theater rather than to try to cope with the additional expenses. In 1902, Irving gave his last performance at his beloved theater.

Irving, Stoker, and the rest of the company made one more American tour. The trip did not go well. Audiences were small, and expenses were high. Irving was still weak from his recent illness. The friendship between Irving and Stoker became strained.

When he returned to England, Irving was content to retire quietly. Fifty-six-year-old Stoker was not. He hoped to get a job as manager of another theater. Nothing was available at the moment, so he concentrated on keeping his name in the public eye. He gave some speeches at schools, and he continued to write.

He finished "The Secret of the Growing Gold," one of his most macabre tales about a murdered woman whose golden hair keeps growing out of the flagstones under which she is buried.

Now free of Lyceum duties, Stoker set himself a goal of writing a book a year. He returned to Cruden Bay where he studied Scottish history, witchcraft, and second sight. He lay in a hammock, surrounded by the sounds of the sea, and there he wrote *Mystery of the Sea*. This novel revolves around the discovery of a great sunken treasure. In this book, as in *Dracula*, Stoker used a first person narrator, and included scenes of madness, and violence. Also as with *Dracula*, Stoker hoped to have *Mystery of the Sea* performed on the stage. To keep this possibility open, he cut and pasted it into a five-act play.

He spent hours in the library, researching Egyptian history to write *The Jewel of the Seven Stars*, a novel about an Egyptian queen's wish for resurrection. This 1903 book is full of fantasy, dreams, and nightmares. Mysteries include a strange birthmark, a seven-clawed creature, a ruby that might have supernatural powers, and experiments in the occult.

In 1904 he completed another novel, *The Man*. The central character is a female named Stephen and the story revolves around her search for her sexual identity. The plot includes a scene in which a large bearded man, perhaps a Stoker-look-alike, rescues a ship in a storm.

Irving never completely recovered from his problems with his lungs and his weakening body. He died in 1905.

Chapter Nine

Life and Writing Slow Down

—Around this time—

Albert Einstein formulated the Special Theory of Relativity.
Lord Baden-Powell founded the Boy Scouts.
General Motors Corporation was formed.
Popular literature included:
Three Lives by Gertrude Stein,
Peter Pan by James Barrie,
The Call of the Wild by Jack London.

Soon after Irving's death, Stoker suffered a stroke that left him weak. While recuperating, he wrote a collection of memories entitled *Personal Reminiscences of Henry Irving*. He focused on Irving as a fine artist who had made the most of his talents. He wrote with admiration for Irving and also with satisfaction for his own role in Irving's life. He used some of his journal notes in the narrative.

Stoker went back to theater management one last time.

He was acting manager for a West End musical of Oliver Goldsmith's *The Vicar of Wakefield*, a story of the misfortunes of a clergyman and his family. The play closed in just two months. After that, Stoker never stayed long on one project. He organized a theatrical exhibition, took part in the Dramatic Debaters (as eagerly as he had debated in Trinity), and became active in a writers' society. He wrote a series of articles on cultural trends including subjects like the possibility of building a national theater, American actors, and censorship. He also gave lectures on Irving throughout England.

In 1906, Stoker suffered another stroke. This one permanently impaired his walk and eyesight. He needed a magnifying glass to help him read and write. His whole body was weak, and he was frequently bedridden.

Dracula still earned royalties, but not enough to provide a living for Stoker and his family. He served for a short time as writer for the *Daily Telegraph*. He wrote some profiles for the *New York World,* including one of Winston Churchill, who later became prime minister of England. He wrote some articles urging book and newspaper publishers to refuse to print "unclean" books and the "foully-conceived novel." In an article for *Nineteenth Century,* he said: "A number of books have been published in England that would be a disgrace to any country . . . the evil is a grave and dangerous one."

In 1908, Stoker worked on two books at once: the fiction *The Lady of the Shroud* and the nonfiction *Famous Imposters*. *The Lady of the Shroud* opens with a report from "The Journal of Occultism," and is written mostly in journal and letter styles. Stoker used material he had learned from Romanian legends and tales including scenes with vampires and coffins. He also used the knowledge he had learned studying the law. He wrote knowledgeably about wills, codicils, testators, and witnesses.

In *Famous Imposters*, Stoker set his theme with the opening sentence: ". . . imposters in one shape or another are likely to flourish as long as human nature remains what it is . . ." The book is in anecdote form, and shows a skill that Stoker learned in his law training, the ability to see both sides of controversial situations.

Stoker had another stroke. Florence took care of him. Noel, now an accountant, was a married man with his own home. Stoker followed the typical regimen for his problem—a little arsenic, strong soups, and no meat. At one time, he wrote to Thornley: "I can now stand for a few seconds at a time on the one leg and better still I am able to work, the book [*Famous Imposters*] is getting on . . . Anyway happy memories are all anyone can ask for."

As soon as he was able, he took up writing again. He had

Bram began suffering a series of strokes as he grew older.

kept notes on misfortunes of his touring company—blizzards, storms, schedule conflicts, and others. Now he included some of these anecdotes in short stories where the characters are passengers stranded on a train because of weather conditions. The characters tell stories to pass the time. Stoker put together these characters and their stories in a collection called *Snowbound: The Record of a Theatrical Touring Party*. This book came out in 1908.

In 1909 he wrote another romantic novel *Lady Athlyne*.

By February 1911, Stoker's health was so poor that he could not write full-time. He requested a grant from the Royal Literary Fund, and he was awarded 100 pounds. Despite this grant, the Stokers could no longer afford to reside in Chelsea where they had lived for thirty years. They took a small flat in London where Stoker sometimes enjoyed short walks along the Thames River.

In March, he began writing *The Lair of the White Worm*. In this novel, he reused some of the research he had done for his earlier works. He recalled his study of electricity and lightning for a character who builds a huge kite. He recalled his fascination with trances for a character who inherits a hypnotist's trunk. Just four months after he started writing it, Stoker finished the book, his eighteenth.

On April 20, 1912 Stoker died at age sixty-four from kidney and other problems. The death certificate listed

Bela Lugosi is one of the actors who played Dracula on the stage and on the screen.

exhaustion as the cause of death. A small group of mourners watched as his ashes were placed in a stone casket.

Obituaries in England and Ireland praised Stoker both for his writing and for his dedication to the stage. A *New York Times* reporter wrote: "[Stoker] wrote fluently and was eagerly interested in all the affairs of the world. Deep down in his nature there was a touch of Celtic mysticism. It sought expression in literary form, but his stories, though they were queer, were not of a memorable quality. His *Life of Irving*, however, is a noteworthy book. He had plenty of friends and enough enemies to indicate that his friendship was worth having. The embodiment of health and strength and geniality, it seems he died too young. He was only sixty-four years of age. Almost every one who knew him will say that he should have lived to be ninety, and kept a young heart in his old age."

Timeline

1847   born in Clontarf, Ireland.

1854   walks for the first time.

1863   enrolls in Trinity College, Dublin.

1871   becomes drama critic for the *Evening Mail;* graduates from Trinity.

1872   sells first short story.

1877   writes first book.

1878   marries Florence Balcombe; becomes stage manager for Lyceum.

1886   begins law studies.

1888   seriously studies Romanian customs and history.

1890   begins writing novel set in Romania.

1897   *Dracula* is published.

1912   dies in England.

Appendix

BRAM STOKER CLUBS
Two of the most active Stoker clubs are:
Count Dracula Fan Club
Penthouse North
29 Washington Square West
New York, NY 10011 - 9180
(President—Dr. Jeanne K. Youngson)

The Bram Stoker Society
Regent House, Trinity College
Dublin 2, Ireland
(President—D. M. Lass)

DRACULA

Dracula is the name of a Slavic ruler who was born in the early 1400s in what is now Romania. Dracula ruled Wallachia, a Romanian province, in the mid 1400s. He was recognized as one of the cruelest tyrants the world had ever known. His record of torture, burning, and murder was believed by some to be unequaled in the history of civilization. Many called him the Impaler because one of his methods of torture was to pierce the bodies of his victims and hang them on stakes around his castle.

Dracula is also a Wallachian word meaning devil. It is used to designate a ruler, particularly of Slavic descent, who is considered to be a tyrant.

Stoker learned about Dracula in part from a book published in 1820, *An Account of the Principalities of Wallachia and Moldavia* by William Wilkinson. At some point in writing his book, Stoker changed the name of his villain from Count Wampyr to Count Dracula.

SOME DRACULA MOVIES

Nosferatu, a silent film made in Germany in 1922. Considered to be one of the greatest horror films of all time.

Dracula, a talking film made in California in 1931. Stars Bela Lugosi as Dracula.

Dracula's Daughter, a Universal film made in 1936. An adaptation of Stoker's story "Dracula's Guest."

Son of Dracula, a Universal film made in 1943. Stars Lon Chaney, Jr. as Count Alucard (this is Dracula spelled backwards).

Drakula Istanbulda, a Turkish film made in 1953. Main setting is Istanbul.

The Return of Dracula, made in USA in 1958. Also released for TV as *The Curse of Dracula*.

The Horror of Dracula, made in England in 1958. Stars Christopher Lee as Dracula.

Dracula—Prince of Darkness, made in England in 1965. A sequel to *Horror of Dracula*

Taste the Blood of Dracula, made in England in 1970. Christopher Lee again plays Dracula.

Dracula's Saga, made in Spain in 1972. Count Dracula seeks mates for his female vampires.

Christopher Lee as Dracula.

In Search of Dracula, made in Sweden in 1972. A Dracula documentary, recalling Vlad the Impaler.

Bram Stoker's Dracula, made in USA in 1973 .A made-for-TV version.

Count Dracula: the True Story, made in Canada. A TV documentary

Bram Stoker's Dracula, made in USA in 1992. Won Oscars for sound, costumes, and make-up.

Dracula: Fact or Fiction?, a documentary made in USA in 1992.

TRANSYLVANIA

Transylvania comprises almost of half of Romania, a country in southeastern Europe. The name of the area can be translated as "land between the forests." The Carpathian Mountains range through Transylvania, creating beautiful scenery sometimes compared to that of the Alps. The mountains create serious transportation and communication problems. The area has experienced a chaotic history of conquerors—Hungarians, Magyars, Turks, Austrians, and others. It was a scene of major campaigns in both World Wars.

Stoker became intrigued with Transylvania at least partly because of Emily Gerard's book *The Land Beyond the Forest* and her article "Transylvanian Superstitions." Gerard wrote: "It would almost seem as though the whole species of demons, pixies, witches, and hobgoblins, driven from the rest of Europe by the wand of science, had taken refuge within this mountain rampart."

VAMPIRES

A vampire is a reanimated corpse. Perhaps people have believed in vampires, for thousands of years. Old Tibetan manuscripts, written around 2500 B.C., tell of blood-sucking creatures with big teeth. The Irish believed in a blood-sucking monster known as "Dearg-dul." Romanians created tales of blood-drinking birds who flew only between sunset and sunrise. Mayans worshiped a bat-like god who sucked blood.

A vampire may take the form of a human or other animal. In *Dracula*, the vampire changes itself into a wolf, a bat, a rat, some mist, and both a young and an old gentleman.

A vampire is neither alive nor dead and is often described as undead. It can be destroyed only by prescribed methods. Two of the most frequently cited methods are cutting off its head and thrusting a stake into its heart. It is said that strings of garlic will ward off the creature.

Victims of vampires become part of an ever-growing circle of creatures which suck blood to maintain their "life" and in the process, create more creatures like themselves.

Bibliography

Auerbach, Nina. *Ellen Terry: Player in Her Time.* New York: W. W. Norton & Company, 1987.

Belford, Barbara. *Bram Stoker: The Biography of the Author of Dracula.* New York: Alfred A. Knopf, 1996.

Farson, Daniel. *The Man Who Wrote Dracula.* New York: St. Martin's Press, 1975.

Gerard, Emily. *The Land Beyond the Forest: Facts, Figures, and Fancies.* New York: Harper & Brothers, 1888.

Kenyon, Fred C. *Hall Caine: The Man and the Novelist.* New York: Haskell House Publisher, Ltd., 1974.

Leatherdale, Clive. *The Origins of Dracula.* London: William Kimber, 1987.

McNally, Raymond and Radu Florescu. *In Search of Dracula.* Boston: Houghton Mifflin Company, 1994.

Melton, J. Gordon. *The Vampire Book: The Encyclopedia of the Undead.* Detroit: Gale Research, Inc., 1994.

Osborne, Charles, ed. *The Bram Stoker Bedside Companion.* New York: Taplinger Publishing Company, 1973.

Rosenbach Museum & Library catalogue for the Centennial Exhibition of *Dracula.* Philadelphia, 1997.

Roth, Phyllis. *Bram Stoker.* Boston: Twayne Publishers, 1982.

Stoker, Bram. *Famous Imposters.* New York: Sturgis & Walton Co., 1910.

Stoker, Bram. *Lair of the White Worm.* London: Rider, 1911.

Stoker, Bram. *Miss Betty.* London: New English Library, no date given.

Stoker, Bram. *The Mystery of the Sea.* New York: Doubleday, 1902.

Stoker, Bram. *Personal Reminisces of Henry Irving,* 2 vols. London: Heinemann, 1906.

Stoker, Bram. *Under the Sunset.* Hollywood: Newcastle Publishing Company, Inc., 1978.

Whitman, Walt. *Leaves of Grass.* New York: Aventine Press, 1931

Wolf, Leonard. *The Essential Dracula.* New York: A Byron Preiss Book, 1975.

Woodham-Smith, Cecil. *The Great Hunger.* New York: Harper & Row, 1962.

Sources

CHAPTER ONE—"Imagination Creates a World"
15 "This early weakness . . ." Stoker, Bram. *Personal Reminiscences of Henry Irving*, p.32
18 "Give me now . . ." Whitman, Walt. *Leaves of Grass*, p.113
18 "Trickle Drops . . ." *Ibid*, p.128
19 "A shroud I see . . ." *Ibid*, p.433

CHAPTER TWO—"The Theater Calls"
24 "Put it [the letter] in your fire . . ." Belford, Barbara. *Bram Stoker*, p.40
24 "I am ugly but strong . . ." Ibid., p.42
26 "I wage a perpetual war . . ." Ibid.
28 "You did well . . ." Ibid.
32 "Irving's physical appearance . . ." Ibid., p.72
32 "I became hysterical . . ." Farson, Daniel, *The Man Who Wrote DRACULA*, p.30

CHAPTER THREE—"Art and Business Meet"
33 "...exquisitely pretty girl . . ." Belford, op.cit., p.85
34 "dry-as-dust" Roth, Phyllis. *Bram Stoker*, p.5-6
34 ". . .a wild, fitful, irresolute . . ." Belford, op.cit., p.80
36 "We understood each other's nature . . ." Ibid.
36 "Will you give up . . ." Osborne, Charles, ed. *The Bram Stoker Bedside Companion*, p.9
40 "Fortunately, for both myself . . ." Stoker, op.cit., p.62
42 "Where are we?" Ibid., p.56
42 "[Irving} gave one . . ." Ibid.

CHAPTER FOUR—"Travels Bring Successes and Trials"
43 ". . . noble and sordid, . . ." Bate, Jonathan and Russell Jackson, eds. *Shakespeare: An Illustrated History*, p. 122
46 "I couldn't myself see . . ." Stoker, op.cit., p.166
46 "...knew that the Giant . . ." Osborne, Charles, ed. op.cit., p.48
48 "...all things lose their being . . ." op.cit., p.81
48 "...the things we do wrong . . ." Belford, op.cit., p.139
48 "...a charming book . . ." Ibid., p.vi
53 "...in three years, I judge . . ." Farson, op.cit., p.74
53 "If I ever do it . . ." Belford, op.cit., p.165

CHAPTER FIVE—"Realism Demands Research"
54 ". . . great shaggy masses . . ." Ibid., p.167
54 ". . . a breath of good, healthy . . ." Ibid., p.168
56 ". . . [it is] deplorable . . ." Farson, op.cit., p.72
56 ". . . we are bound . . ." Ibid., p.78
58 ". . . twenty years ago, electric energy . . ." Stoker, op.cit., p.176
60 "And sitting on the head . . ." Osborne, op.cit., p.127
61 ". . . as the smoke cleared . . ." Belford, op.cit., p.179
61 ". . . [clouds] so dank and damp and cold . . ." Ibid., p.194
62 ". . . about a hundred lines in all . . ." Ibid., p.198

CHAPTER SIX—"Writing Competes with the Theater"
63 "Venice, a Public Place" Stoker, op.cit., p.293
64 "Go back to your seat." Farson, op.cit., p.58
65 "When shall we three meet again . . ." Hunter, G.K., ed. *Macbeth*, p.53
66 "I often say to myself . . ." Auerbach, Nina. *Ellen Terry: Player in Her Time*, p.89
66 ". . . the indolent charm . . . companions" Gerard, Emily. *The Land Beyond the Forest*, p.1
68 "In very obstinate cases . . ." Gerard, op.cit., p.185
69 "Dracula in Wallachian ...brink of precipice . . ." McNally, Raymond and Radu Florescu, *The Essential Dracula*, p.49
70 ". . . the *penangulan* takes possession . . . then flower " Ibid., p.192
72 "I sat next to him . . ." Belford, op.cit., p.238
74 "The red glare of the sunset . . ." Stoker, Bram. *Miss Betty*, p.100
74 "I would like . . ." Stoker, Bram, *Personal Reminisces of Henry Irving*, p.195

CHAPTER SEVEN—"Count Dracula Casts His Spell"
76 "Cool it with . . . baboon's blood." Ibid., p.137
76 "All shall be well . . ." Ibid.
77 ". . . [his] duties are to see . . ." Ibid., p.302
77 ". . . the journey-wolves howl . . ." Exhibition Catalogue of Rosenbach Museum & Library, p.29
78 "I really think . . ." Farson, op.cit., p.62
78 ". . . a mass that in the gloom . . ." Osborne, ed., op.cit., p.222
79 "The history of the time . . ." Stoker, Bram, op.cit., p.266-67
80 "Aug. 11 bat outside . . . Jonathan at hospital" McNally, op.cit., 103, 109
82 "Suddenly I felt a hand. . ." Shelly, Mary et al., *Frankenstein, Dracula, Mr. Jekyll and Mr. Hyde*, p.34
82 "He disgusted me . . ." Ibid., p.78
82 "I found my dear one . . ." Ibid., p.113

CHAPTER EIGHT—"A Writing Career Flourishes"
85 "Dreadful!" Rosenbach catalogue op.cit., p.31
86 ". . . the book is necessarily full . . ." Ibid., p.33
86 "My dear, it is splended. . ." Ibid.
86 "in a nightmarish dream . . ." Ibid., p.256
86 ". . . reads at times like . . ." Rosenbach, op.cit., p.33
86 ". . . a powerful and horrible . . ." Osborne, ed., op.cit., p.11
86 "Trees are trees . . ." Belford, op. cit., p.220
89 ". . . pretty much the same . . .", Ibid., p.282
90 "Splash! My feet had given way . . ." Osborne, ed., op.cit., p.92
90 ". . . at times we rolled . . ." Belford, op.cit., p.286
91 ". . . a great shambling, good-natured . . ." Ibid., p.288

CHAPTER NINE—"Life and Writing Slow Down"
95 ". . . unclean . . . foully-conceived novel . . ." Ibid,, p.312
95 "A number of books . . ." Osborne, ed., op.cit., p.13
96 ". . . imposters in one shape . . ." Roth, op.cit., p.129
96 "I can now stand . . ." Belford, op.cit., p.315
100 "[Stoker] wrote fluently and was . . ." *New York Times*, April 23, 1912, p.12

Index